FINDING A VOICE:
Women's Fight for Equality in U.S. Society

WOMEN IN THE CIVIL RIGHTS MOVEMENT

JUDY L. HASDAY

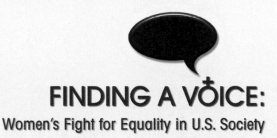

FINDING A VOICE:
Women's Fight for Equality in U.S. Society

TITLES IN THIS SERIES

WOMEN IN THE CIVIL RIGHTS MOVEMENT

JUDY L. HASDAY

MASON CREST
PHILADELPHIA

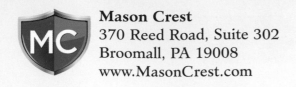

Mason Crest
370 Reed Road, Suite 302
Broomall, PA 19008
www.MasonCrest.com

Printed and bound in the United States of America.

CPSIA Compliance Information: Batch #FF2012-7. For further information, contact Mason Crest at 1-866-MCP-Book.

First printing
1 3 5 7 9 8 6 4 2

Library of Congress Cataloging-in-Publication Data

Hasday, Judy L., 1957-
  Women in the civil rights movement / Judy L. Hasday.
     p. cm. — (Finding a voice : women's fight for equality in U.S. society)
  Includes bibliographical references and index.
  ISBN 978-1-4222-2356-7 (hc)
  ISBN 978-1-4222-2366-6 (pb)
1. African American women civil rights workers—Juvenile literature. 2. Women civil rights workers—Juvenile literature. 3. Civil rights movements—United States—History—Juvenile literature. 4. African Americans—Civil rights—History—Juvenile literature. I. Title.
  E185.61.H357 2012
  323.1196'073—dc23

                              2011043481

Publisher's note: All quotations in this book are taken from original sources, and contain the spelling and grammatical inconsistencies of the original texts.

Picture credits: Time & Life Pictures/Getty Images: 41; courtesy Lyndon B. Johnson Presidential Library: 3, 53; Library of Congress: 8, 12, 13, 14, 16, 17, 18, 20, 21, 23, 25, 26, 27, 28, 31, 37, 38, 45, 46, 48, 50, 51, 56, 57; © 2011 Photos.com, a division of Getty Images: 10; Wikimedia Commons: 33, 39.

TABLE OF CONTENTS

INTRODUCTION

A. Page Harrington, director, Sewall-Belmont House & Museum

As the Executive Director of the Sewall-Belmont House & Museum, which is the fifth and final headquarters of the historic National Woman's Party (NWP), I am surrounded each day by artifacts that give voice to the stories of Alice Paul, Lucy Burns, Doris Stevens, Alva Belmont, and the whole community of women who waged an intense campaign for the right to vote during the second decade of the 20th century. The original photographs, documents, protest banners, and magnificent floor-length capes worn by these courageous activists during marches and demonstrations help us bring their work to life for the many groups who tour the museum each week.

The perseverance of the suffragists bore fruit in 1920, with the ratification of the 19th Amendment. It was a huge milestone, though certainly not the end of the journey toward full equality for American women.

Throughout much (if not most) of American history, social conventions and the law constrained female participation in the political, economic, and intellectual life of the nation. Women's voices were routinely stifled, their contributions downplayed or dismissed, their potential ignored. Underpinning this state of affairs was a widely held assumption of male superiority in most spheres of human endeavor.

Always, however, there were women who gave the lie to gender-based stereotypes. Some helped set the national agenda. For example, in the years preceding the Revolutionary War, Mercy Otis Warren made a compelling case for American independence through her writings. Abigail Adams, every bit the intellectual equal of her husband, counseled John Adams to "remember the ladies and be more generous and favorable to them than your ancestors" when creating laws for the new country. Sojourner Truth helped lead the movement to abolish slavery in the 19th century. A hundred years later, Rosa Parks galvanized the civil rights movement, which finally secured for African Americans the promise of equality under the law.

The lives of these women are familiar today. So, too, are the stories of groundbreakers such as astronaut Sally Ride; Supreme Court justice Sandra Day O'Connor; and Nancy Pelosi, Speaker of the House of Representatives.

But famous figures are only part of the story. The path toward gender equality was also paved—and American society shaped—by countless women whose individual lives and deeds have never been chronicled in depth. These include the women who toiled alongside their fathers and brothers and husbands on the western frontier; the women who kept U.S. factories running during World War II; and the women who worked tirelessly to promote the goals of the modern feminist movement.

The FINDING A VOICE series tells the stories of famous and anonymous women alike. Together these volumes provide a wide-ranging overview of American women's long quest to achieve full equality with men—a quest that continues today.

The Sewall-Belmont House & Museum is located at 144 Constitution Avenue in Washington, D.C. You can find out more on the Web at www.sewallbelmont.org

For many years in the United States, African Americans suffered discrimination because of their race. (Left) A "colored" water fountain outside the courthouse of a North Carolina town. (Bottom) A black man climbs the steps to the "colored" entrance at the rear of a movie theater in Mississippi. The lower door is labled "white men only."

1

SLAVERY AND SEGREGATION

Throughout the history of the United States, women have struggled to gain full equality with men. They have fought for an equal education, the right to cast votes, and the opportunity to hold certain jobs. This ongoing fight for equality has brought women of all races and religions together in a "sisterhood" effort that has been a remarkable force for change.

However, one segment of the sisterhood has had an additional struggle. African American women have had to work for the rights and freedoms denied them because of the color of their skin. Their battle against racism has its roots in the past.

SLAVERY

From the 16th to the 19th centuries, about 645,000 African slaves were brought to the colonies in North America. Referred to as "colored people," they were held against their will and separated from their families. They were treated as property instead of human beings and forced to work as laborers without any compensation.

At the end of the American Revolutionary War (1775–1783) the practice of slavery was on the decline in the northern part of the United States.

Slaves pick cotton on a Southern plantation, 1850s. When the Civil War began in 1861, nearly 4 million African Americans were held in slavery. Their labor fueled the South's economy, which was based on cash crops like cotton, tobacco, and rice.

During the first half of the 19th century, the economy of the northern states came to focus more on factories that produced textiles, shoes, and finished goods. By 1804, many of the northern states had made slavery illegal. But slavery continued in the southern states, where economic growth came from agriculture. Plantation owners depended on slave labor to produce crops of tobacco, sugar cane, coffee, and cotton. In 1800 there were about a million slaves in the United States. By 1860 the number of slaves in the South had increased to nearly 4 million.

THE ABOLITIONIST MOVEMENT

The call to end slavery in America began as early as 1688. That is when Quakers living in Germantown, Pennsylvania (now part of the city of Philadelphia), petitioned leaders of their church to outlaw the practice.

Quakers were members of the Society of Friends, a religious group that believed in the equality of all people—male and female, black and white. Many of its members wanted to abolish, or end slavery. They were called abolitionists. They spoke out against the slave trade. And they boycotted products created by slave labor.

Over the years, the call for the end of slavery gained many supporters. Much of that support, however, came from people living in the northern states. In Boston, social reformer, journalist, and abolitionist William Lloyd Garrison founded an antislavery newspaper in the 1830s. He called it *The Liberator*. He also lectured against slavery. In one speech he said:

> I am a believer in that portion of the Declaration of American Independence in which it is set forth, as among self-evident truths, "that all men are created equal; that they are endowed by their Creator with certain inalienable rights; that among these are life, liberty, and the pursuit of happiness." Hence, I am an Abolitionist. Hence, I cannot but regard oppression in every form—and most of all, that which turns a man into a thing—with indignation and abhorrence.

Garrison also founded the American Anti-Slavery Society. One of its key leaders was Frederick Douglass. An escaped slave, Douglass was a power-

FAST FACT

English pottery manufacturer Josiah Wedgwood produced an emblem of the antislavery campaign in 1787. The medallion showed a kneeling African man in chains. It asked, "Am I Not a Man and a Brother?" A later image showed a female slave, and asked the question, "Am I Not a Woman and a Sister?"

ful antislavery speaker and writer. Women also were members of the Society. Among the well-known white female abolitionists were Maria Weston Chapman, Abby Kelley Foster, Lydia Maria Child, and Lucy Stone. They lectured or worked with black women in an effort to end slavery.

AFRICAN-AMERICAN WOMEN ABOLITIONISTS

One lecturer against slavery was a black woman named Maria Stewart. In the early 1830s Boston, she gave speeches to African American audiences. She called on them to help end slavery. And she asked them to refuse to accept racial inequality. Stewart is believed to have been the first American woman of any color or ethnicity to lecture about political issues in a public forum. But she lectured for only a few years. Afterward she continued to work for antislavery groups.

Abolitionist Sojourner Truth (1797?–1883) was also an advocate of the women's rights movement. She is best known for her 1851 speech "Ain't I a Woman?" delivered at the Ohio Woman's Rights Convention in Akron, Ohio.

Unlike Stewart, former slave Sojourner Truth spent decades on the lecture circuit. She drew large crowds wherever she took to the stage. During the 1840s and 1850s, she spoke the "Truth" about the wrongs of slavery. Truth spent her adult life speaking and working tirelessly to bring an end to the practice.

Another well-known black lecturer was Frances Ellen Watkins Harper. During the 1850s the writer and teacher often spoke out against slavery. She also helped runaway slaves escape to Canada via the Underground Railroad. This was a large

Harriet Tubman (1820?–1913) was nick-named "Moses" for her furtive work help-ing African-American slaves escape to the North during the 1850s and 1860s. During the Civil War, Tubman worked as a spy for the Union Army and guided Union troops during an 1863 raid of plantations on the Combahee River in South Carolina that freed some 700 slaves. Later, during the 1890s, Tubman worked with Susan B. Anthony and other Suffragists who sought the right for women to vote.

network of people who provided food and shelter to slaves seeking freedom.

A famous "conductor" on the Underground Railroad was Harriet Tubman. Born a slave in Maryland's Dorchester County, she was in her late twenties when she escaped from slavery in 1849. Tubman then returned to the South to lead other blacks to freedom. Over a 10-year period, she made the dangerous trip south 19 times. She ultimately helped more than 300 slaves reach the North. During the 1950s she also gave testimony at anti-slavery lectures of her experiences as a slave. Fellow abolitionist Frederick Douglass once said of Tubman, "Excepting John Brown . . . I know of no one who has willingly encountered more perils and hardships to serve our enslaved people than [Harriet Tubman]."

WAR AND RECONSTRUCTION

The continued practice of slavery led to the U.S. Civil War. This conflict between the North and South raged from 1861 to 1865. Before the war

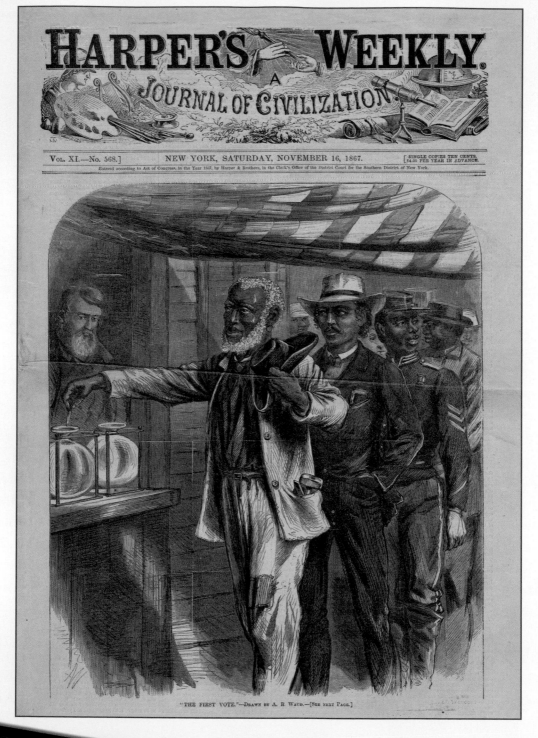

"THE FIRST VOTE."—DRAWN BY A. R. WAUD.—[SEE NEXT PAGE.]

ended, Congress passed the Thirteenth Amendment to the Constitution. When ratified at the end of 1865, it abolished slavery in the United States.

Other amendments soon followed. In 1868 Congress sought to guarantee blacks due process and equal protection under the law by passing the Fourteenth Amendment. The Fifteenth Amendment, passed in 1870, gave blacks the right to vote. It stated that all male U.S. citizens had this right regardless of their "race, color, or previous condition of servitude."

RACIAL SEGREGATION

A period known as the Reconstruction Era (1866–1877) followed the Civil War. During this time, the country worked to rebuild. The federal government also tried to protect the freedoms of former slaves. But in the South, whites resisted. Many Southern state and local legislatures imposed legal restrictions on blacks. These laws were known as the Black Codes. The laws took away many legal rights of blacks. They could not testify against whites. They could not vote, hold office, or serve on juries.

By the end of Reconstruction, the Black Codes had been replaced by Jim Crow laws. These laws prevented whites and blacks from coming in contact with one another in public facilities. "Whites Only" and "Colored Only" signs hung over separate door entrances and exits. There were separate public restrooms, hospitals, schools, and churches. In trains, black passengers had to ride in separate cars from whites. Jim Crow laws also established literacy tests and poll taxes. These restrictions were to prevent African Americans from voting.

(Opposite) This illustration on the cover of *Harper's Weekly*, a popular magazine of the 1860s and 1870s, shows a line of African-American men preparing to cast ballots in an election. The first man is dressed as a laborer, the second is dressed as a businessman, the third is wearing a Union army uniform, and the fourth appears to be dressed as a farmer. The Fifteenth Amendment to the U.S. Constitution, ratified in 1870, made it illegal to deny a citizen the right to vote based on that person's "race, color, or previous condition of servitude." Although the amendment permitted African-American men to vote, black and white women would not be guaranteed that right for another 50 years.

BLACK WOMEN'S CLUB MOVEMENT

Numerous black women's clubs formed during the 1800s. Some were social clubs. Others were professional clubs or church groups. These groups worked

Ida Wells-Barnett

for various causes. Some focused on improving education in the black community. Others sought to improve conditions for women. Still others worked to win women the right to vote. (Women would not achieve that right until August 1920. That was when the Nineteenth Amendment was ratified.)

Women's clubs gained political power when they joined together. Josephine St. Pierre Ruffin (1842–1924) is credited with organizing the first national convention of black women's clubs. "Our woman's movement is a woman's movement in that it is led and directed by women," Ruffin said at the 1895 Boston meeting. That convention led to the formation of a national organization.

In 1896 activists Ida B. Wells-Barnett, Mary Church Terrell, and Frances Ellen Watkins Harper helped form the National Association of Colored Women (NACW). This group worked to promote suffrage for women. It also campaigned against lynching. And it opposed Jim Crow laws.

Mary Church Terrell served as the first president of the National Association of Colored Women. Other founders included Margaret Murray Washington, Fanny Jackson Coppin,

Mary Church Terrell

Charlotte Forten Grimké, and Harriet Tubman. By 1910, the NACW claimed a membership of 50,000. It was later known as the National Council of Negro Women.

During the 1860s and early 1870s, some people in the southern states joined groups like the Ku Klux Klan (pictured), the White League, and the Red Shirts. These groups attacked and terrorized African-American voters, as well as those whites who supported them, in an attempt to keep them from voting.

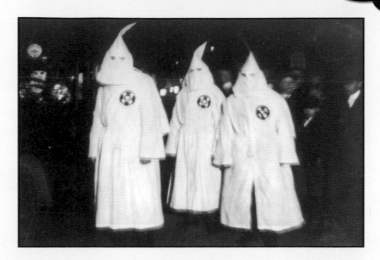

Blacks who protested were often threatened and beaten. Some were murdered by hostile mobs in brutal lynchings. According to statistics collected by the Tuskeegee Institute, over 3,400 African Americans were lynched in the United States between 1882 and 1951. (The actual number of lynchings may actually be higher. Because mob lynchings were murders by citizens, many cases went unreported each year.) Many blacks fell victim to white segregationist groups like the Ku Klux Klan (KKK).

THE "SEPARATE BUT EQUAL" DOCTRINE

In 1890 Louisiana legislators passed the Separate Car Act. It called for separate accommodations for blacks and whites on trains. The following

FAST FACT

According to the Tuskeegee Institute, the highest number of lynchings occurred in 1892, when 161 African Americans were lynched. Sixty-nine whites were also lynched that year. Attacks on whites took place mostly in western states, while lynchings of blacks predominantly occurred in the southern states.

FAST FACT

In 1913 Ida B. Wells-Barnett founded the first organization for black women working to obtain the vote for women. It was called the Alpha Suffrage Club of Chicago.

year a group of prominent African American men met in New Orleans. Known as the Comité des Citoyens, or Citizen's Committee, the group of men decided to challenge the Louisiana law.

The group selected a 30-year-old shoemaker named Homer Plessy to board a train in New Orleans and sit in one of the rail cars assigned for white passengers. Plessy was arrested, and found guilty of breaking the law. The case was appealed to the U.S. Supreme Court.

In 1896 the Court ruled on *Plessy v. Ferguson*. It found that the states had the right to maintain "separate but equal" public facilities. That decision meant racial segregation was legal. In the years to come, the Plessy case would be used to argue against any future segregation cases brought before the courts.

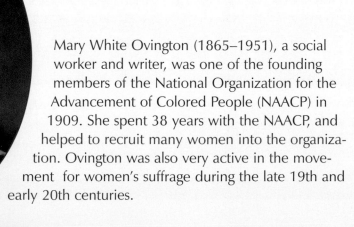

Mary White Ovington (1865–1951), a social worker and writer, was one of the founding members of the National Organization for the Advancement of Colored People (NAACP) in 1909. She spent 38 years with the NAACP, and helped to recruit many women into the organization. Ovington was also very active in the movement for women's suffrage during the late 19th and early 20th centuries.

2

INTEGRATING
THE SCHOOLS

At the turn of the 20th century, Jim Crow laws legally segregated whites and blacks in the South. But racial discrimination also existed in the North. There, many blacks were unable to get a decent education or jobs. Organizations that worked for the civil rights of African Americans soon formed. In 1909 the National Association for the Advancement of Colored People (NAACP) was founded. It worked within the legal and court system to achieve equal rights for blacks. A year later the National Urban League was established.

Although women had earned the right to vote in 1920, black women—like black men—were prevented from exercising that right. Taxes, registration restrictions, and threats prevented African Americans from voting. Jim Crow laws also imposed literacy tests that few blacks could pass. Most blacks could not read and write because the separate schools for African Americans provided an inadequate education. They were overcrowded, rundown, and poorly funded.

DESEGREGATION

During the 1930s the NAACP launched an effort to achieve equality in schools. This involved filing lawsuits demanding that the educational facilities provided for black students be made equal to those for whites. Some

Attorney Constance Baker Motley (1921–2005) began her career with the NAACP's legal department. She later became the first African-American woman elected to the New York state senate.

of these suits proved successful. But the overall goal of the NAACP was to end legal segregation altogether.

A team of NAACP lawyers, headed by Legal Defense and Educational Fund head Thurgood Marshall, prepared several lawsuits to challenge the *Plessy* doctrine. In December 1952 there were five school segregation lawsuits awaiting review by the U.S. Supreme Court. They represented more than 150 plaintiffs who were from several different states. All challenged the lawfulness of racial segregation practices in the public school system. The Court consolidated all five cases under one name: *Oliver Brown et al. v. the Board of Education of Topeka, Kansas*.

Lawyer Constance Baker Motley worked as the NAACP Legal Defense Fund associate counsel. In this role she helped write the summary of facts for the Brown case. Motley would later become a state senator and federal judge.

THE END OF "SEPARATE BUT EQUAL"

NAACP attorneys, including Thurgood Marshall, presented their arguments in *Brown v. Board of Education* on December 9, 1952. The lawyers argued that school segregation violated the "equal protection clause" of the 14th Amendment. This clause prohibits states from denying citizens equal treatment under the law. To support their case, the lawyers presented evidence that segregated schools had a negative impact on African American students. The schools caused black children to believe they were not equal to whites. Segregation laws in education resulted in a separate and unequal education for black children.

The Supreme Court heard the case again on two more occasions. In May 1954 it submitted its decision. The Court agreed that segregation in public education violated the equal protection clause of the 14th Amendment. In announcing the unanimous decision, Chief Justice Earl Warren wrote:

> Segregation of white and colored children in public schools has a detrimental effect upon the colored children. The impact is greater when it has the sanction of the law. . . . We conclude that, in the field of public education, the doctrine of "separate but equal" has no place. Separate educational facilities are inherently unequal.

The Supreme Court ruled that racially segregated public schools were a violation of the U.S. Constitution. All public schools were ordered to desegregate.

THE CHALLENGE BEGINS

The *Brown v. Board of Education* decision gave the civil rights movement a defining victory. However, the process of desegregating schools would take determination and time. The order to integrate public schools met with heavy resistance from Southern whites. It wasn't uncommon for resolute segregationists to refuse

Four of the five plaintiffs in the cases consolidated under *Brown v. Board of Education*: (front, left to right) Linda Brown Smith (*Brown v. Board of Education of Topeka*), Ethel Louise Belton Brown (*Gebhart v. Belton*), (back) Harry Briggs, Jr. (*Briggs v. Elliot*), and Spottswood Bolling Jr. (*Bolling v. Sharpe*). The fifth case was *Dorothy E. Davis v. County School Board of Prince Edward County, Virginia.*

FAST FACT

Two NAACP lawyers working on the *Brown v. Board of Education* case rose to prominence. In 1966 Constance Baker Motley became the first African American woman nominated to the federal judiciary. In 1967 Thurgood Marshall became the nation's first black Supreme Court justice.

to integrate their public schools. Opposition came from public schools all over the South, from Texas and Kentucky to Tennessee and Mississippi.

Resistance took many forms. Rather than integrate, some white-dominated school boards closed schools. In other cases, mobs of angry whites prevented African American students from attempting to enter all-white schools. Some government officials openly opposed integration. They refused to enforce the ruling.

In Kentucky, Governor A. B. Chandler fully complied with the Court's ruling. He ordered the desegregation of the public schools. And he called on the state's National Guard to ensure a safe and nonviolent transition in the integration process. Chandler defended his position by saying, "Mobs led by bad tempered men were taking over. You can't let mobs enforce the law. The rights of people were at stake."

THE LITTLE ROCK NINE

In Little Rock, the capital city of Arkansas, NAACP branch president Daisy Bates and her husband, L. C. Gatson, welcomed news of the *Brown v. Board of Education* decision. The couple published a pro-civil rights newspaper. Called the *Arkansas State Press*, it carried stories of injustices against African Americans. Bates was a longtime member of the NAACP. She and other activists were determined to see integration take place in the city's public schools.

The Little Rock NAACP branch selected nine black teenagers to integrate the city's all-white Central High School. Bates provided support for the six girls (Minnijean Brown, Elizabeth Eckford, Thelma Mothershed, Melba Pattillo, Gloria Ray, and Carlotta Walls) and the three boys (Ernest Green, Terrence Roberts, and Jefferson Thomas). They would soon be known as the Little Rock Nine.

Activist Daisy Bates (1914–1999), who coordinated the integration of Little Rock's Central High School in 1957–58, is pictured with the "Little Rock Nine": (front, left to right) Thelma Mothershed, Minnijean Brown, Elizabeth Eckford, Gloria Ray, (back) Jefferson Thomas, Melba Pattillo, Terrence Roberts, Carlotta Walls, Bates, and Ernest Green.

FAST FACT

Little Rock Nine student Ernest Green served as assistant secretary of Housing and Urban Affairs during the administration of President Jimmy Carter (1977–1981).

On September 2, 1957, Arkansas governor Orval Faubus announced that he would defy the federal order to desegregate the schools in Little Rock. He called out the Arkansas National Guard.

Two days later, on September 4, the nine African-American teens tried to report to Central High School. The students were supposed to arrive together, but Elizabeth Eckford had not gotten the message. When she approached the school alone, she was turned away by the guardsmen. All nine teenagers were prevented from entering the school. White segregationists spit on the students, screamed insults, and threatened their lives. Photos of Eckford being taunted by whites as she tried to leave appeared in the national press. Media reports showed millions of Americans around the country the ugliness of racial prejudice.

When Governor Faubus called up the National Guard to prevent the African American students from entering the school, Bates and others went to the federal authorities. Calling the mob behavior "disgraceful," President Eisenhower took action. He dispatched members of the 101st

FAST FACT

In a November 1999 ceremony, each member of the Little Rock Nine was awarded the Congressional Gold Medal. It is the highest civilian award given by the U.S. Congress.

A Washington, D.C., high-school classroom that was integrated in the wake of the *Brown v. Board of Education* ruling, 1957.

Airborne Division to protect the Little Rock Nine. On September 25, Daisy Bates accompanied the nine students as the federal troops escorted them into Central High School.

Despite several months of ongoing harassment, eight of the nine students managed to complete their school year. In 1958 Ernest Green became the first African American to graduate from Central High. The Little Rock Nine would be remembered for the dignity and courage they displayed in troubling times. Their success in integrating the all-white school meant the days of school segregation had come to an end.

NAACP AND DESEGREGATION

The *Brown v. Board of Education* decision did not put an end to segregation in other public areas. There were still whites-only restaurants, movie theaters, and restrooms. NAACP lawyers continued to challenge segregation in the courts.

One of the civil rights group's leading lawyers was Juanita Jackson Mitchell. She was the first black woman to practice law in Maryland. After earning her law degree in 1950, she began working at the NAACP Baltimore, Maryland, office. Her efforts helped open up schools and other public places to blacks. She is also credited with helping make Maryland

ELLA JO BAKER (1903–1986)

Ella Josephine Baker was active in the civil rights movement for more than 50 years. She worked with many important leaders, including W. E. B. Du Bois, Thurgood Marshall, and Martin Luther King. She also worked with civil rights activists Rosa Parks and Diane Nash.

Baker was born in 1903 in Norfolk, Virginia. She grew up in North Carolina. In 1927, she graduated from Shaw University, in Raleigh. After moving to New York City, Baker worked in Harlem as a community organizer. In the early 1940s, she joined the NAACP as an assistant field secretary. Much of her work involved fundraising and organizing membership campaigns in the South.

Baker helped establish other civil rights organizations. In 1957 she set up the headquarters of the newly formed Southern Christian Leadership Conference (SCLC) in Atlanta, Georgia. In April 1960, she organized a conference that led to the founding of the Student Nonviolent Coordinating Committee (SNCC). She also served as an advisor to the SNCC for several years.

Baker received little public recognition for her work. But she claimed that did not bother her. "The movement of the '50's and '60's was carried largely by women," she once said. "It was sort of second nature to women to play a supportive role."

In January 1937 Juanita Jackson (1913–1992), the NAACP's first national youth director, visited the Scottsboro Boys, a group of African-Americans who were falsely convicted of raping two white women and unjustly sentenced to long prison terms. She led a national campaign to raise money for their defense. Jackson, who married fellow civil rights activist Clarence Mitchell Jr. in 1938, served as director of the NAACP's Baltimore office from 1950 to 1978.

the first southern state to integrate its school system.

Many women worked for the NAACP in other capacities. Some served as coordinators of membership drives. Others worked in administrative roles or as branch directors. One dedicated NAACP worker was Ella Jo Baker. She joined in the organization in 1940 as a field secretary. By 1943 she had become a branch director, and at the time the highest-ranking woman in the NAACP. Later, as president of the New York branch of the NAACP, Baker was active in efforts to help New York City schools integrate after the *Brown v. Board of Education* decision.

THE BUS STOP
The Montgomery Bus Boycott

At the stop on this site on December 1, 1955, Mrs. Rosa Parks boarded the bus which would transport her name into history. Returning home after a long day working as a seamstress for Montgomery Fair department store, she refused the bus driver's order to give up her seat to boarding whites. Her arrest, conviction, and fine launched the Montgomery Bus Boycott. The Boycott began December 5, the day of Parks's trial, as a protest by African-Americans for unequal treatment they received on the bus line. Refusing to ride the buses, they maintained the Boycott until the U.S. Supreme Court ordered integration of public transportation one year later. Dr. Martin Luther King, Jr. led the Boycott, the beginning of the modern Civil Rights Movement.

SPONSORED BY ALPHA KAPPA ALPHA SORORITY, INCORPORATED DURING ITS CENTENNIAL SALUTE
ALABAMA HISTORICAL ASSOCIATION 2008

At this spot on Dexter Avenue in Montgomery, Alabama, a woman named Rosa Parks waited to board a city bus on December 1, 1955. Her bus ride that day would turn out to be a pivotal moment in the civil rights movement.

3

THE MONTGOMERY BUS BOYCOTT

Jim Crow laws affected African Americans all over the United States. Many states and cities had laws that punished businesses that did not provide separate facilities for black and white customers. Some state laws prohibited interracial marriages. Others imposed segregation practices in public transportation.

In Montgomery, Alabama, city law required passengers on buses to be segregated. Whites took seats in the front rows. African Americans had to take seats in the back of the bus. If the bus became full, all the blacks in the row nearest the white section had to get up from their seats. This would create a new row for white passengers. If there were no seats available for them, African American riders were supposed to stand. In addition, black passengers often had to board the bus in the front door to pay the fare. But then they had to exit the bus and reenter using the rear door.

DEFYING THE LAW

One of the many blacks who rode the city buses in 1955 was Rosa Parks. She had grown up in Montgomery. So she was no stranger to injustices against African Americans. "Back then, we didn't have any civil rights," she would later recall. "It was just a matter of survival, of existing from one day to the next. I remember going to sleep as a girl hearing the Klan ride at night and hearing a lynching and being afraid the house would burn down."

Parks had joined the Montgomery chapter of the NAACP in 1943. And she served as a part-time secretary in the office. She also worked as a seamstress at a department store.

On December 1, 1955, after a long day at work, Parks boarded a Montgomery city bus driven by James F. Blake. She sat down in the first row of the seats designated for African Americans. At the next stop, several whites boarded the bus. They filled all the whites-only seats. One white man was left standing. Blake ordered Parks and three other African Americans to give up from their seats so the white man could sit down.

Rosa Parks refused. She was arrested for violating the city law. Years later she explained why she remained seated:

> [W]hen that white driver stepped back toward us, when he waved his hand and ordered us up and out of our seats, I felt a determination cover my body like a quilt on a winter night. I felt all the meanness of every white driver I'd seen who'd been ugly to me and other black people through the years I'd known on the buses in Montgomery. I felt a light suddenly shine through the darkness.

Edgar Daniel "E. D." Nixon was head of the Montgomery NAACP chapter. He and Clifford and Virginia Durr paid Parks's bail. She was released from jail. But her arrest outraged African Americans all over the city.

BUS BOYCOTT

It was not the first time that an African American had been arrested for refusing to give up a seat on a bus in Montgomery. But civil rights activists believed that Rosa Park's arrest marked a turning point. They had been waiting for the right moment to initiate a boycott of the buses.

The majority of the city's bus passengers were African Americans. If blacks refused to ride the buses, the buses could not continue to operate.

Rosa Parks (1913–2005) is fingerprinted by a Montgomery police officer after her arrest. Her act of civil disobedience inspired African Americans to seek the full rights of American citizens. Parks has been called the "mother of the civil rights movement."

African Americans could send a powerful message to authorities that blacks deserved to be treated the same as whites.

One of Montgomery's activists was Women's Political Council president and college teacher Jo Ann Robinson. She had firsthand experience with bus segregation. In 1949 she had been verbally attacked by a bus driver for accidentally sitting in the wrong section of bus. Angry and embarrassed, Robinson had vowed to work to end bus segregation in the city.

FAST FACT

Section 11 of the Chapter 6, Montgomery, Alabama, City Code of 1952 gave city bus operators the legal powers of a police officer. The statute allowed drivers to assign seats based on race.

After Parks's act of civil disobedience, the Women's Political Council called for a boycott of city buses. Robinson and two coworkers prepared 35,000 copies of a flyer to deliver to black households. The flyer asked African Americans to stop riding the buses the following Monday. That was the day Rosa Parks was due in court. The flyer read:

> This is for Monday, Dec. 5, 1955 — Another Negro woman has been arrested and thrown into jail because she refused to get up out of her seat on the bus and give it to a white person. . . . This has to be stopped. . . . We are therefore asking every Negro to stay off the buses Monday in protest of the arrest and trial. Don't ride the buses to work, to town, to school, or anywhere on Monday.

The Sunday edition of the *Montgomery Advertiser* carried the boycott story its front page. And several members of the local clergy reinforced requests for blacks to participate in the boycott. One of them was Martin Luther King Jr. He was the new minister of the Dexter Avenue Baptist Church. King's leadership in the Montgomery bus boycott would bring him national attention.

King would later recall that on the morning of December 5 his wife Coretta called him to the living room. She wanted him to look out the window. As Martin approached the window, he saw a bus slowly riding past their house. The vehicle was empty. Soon another bus passed by. It too was empty.

Activists had initially planned for the boycott to last only one day. But because of its success, they decided to continue the protest. Instead of riding buses, Montgomery's black residents walked, carpooled, and took cabs.

LEGAL CHALLENGE

After Parks's arrest, four other women who had been arrested on city buses agreed to serve as plaintiffs in a lawsuit that challenged city and state segregation laws. In February 1956, as the bus boycott continued to empty city buses, *Browder v. Gayle* was filed in U.S. district court.

The suit charged that Alabama's bus segregation laws violated the 14th Amendment of the Constitution. And on December 17, the U.S. Supreme Court agreed. The Court's ruling on *Browder v. Gayle* invalidated the state and city laws.

Only then were Montgomery civil rights activists willing to call off the bus boycott. It officially ended on December 20, 1956. The protest had lasted 381 days.

TURNING POINT

Many people consider the success of the Montgomery bus boycott as the birth of the civil rights movement. The nonviolent, unified protest inspired the formation in February 1957 of a new civil rights organization. The Southern Christian Leadership Conference (SCLC) was founded by African American ministers. Its first president was Martin Luther King Jr.

Several men and women involved in the boycott would go on to become prominent leaders in the civil rights movement. They included Rosa Parks,

Rosa Parks was riding National City Lines transit bus #2857 when she was arrested. Today, the restored bus is on exhibit at the Henry Ford Museum in Dearborn, Michigan.

Ralph Abernathy, Fred Gray, Clifford and Virginia Durr, Jo Ann Robinson, and Andrew Young. The success of the bus boycott showed blacks that by working together, they could bring about change.

In 1958 King wrote about the boycott in his book *Stride Toward Freedom*. "The story of Montgomery is the story of 50,000 Negroes who are tired of injustice and oppression," he wrote. "[A]nd who are willing to substitute tired feet for tired souls and walk and walk until the walls of injustice are crushed by the battering rams of historical necessity." King noted in his book, "We came to see that, in the long run, it is more honorable to walk in dignity than ride in humiliation."

BROWDER V. GAYLE

In *Browder v. Gayle*, four women challenged the segregation policy on Montgomery's public buses. They were Aurelia Browder, Susie McDonald, Claudette Colvin, and Mary Louise Smith. The case is named for Browder, who was the lead petitioner, and William A. Gayle, who was the mayor of the city of Montgomery.

The women represented different generations. But all had been mistreated or arrested for breaking city bus segregation laws. Claudette Colvin was just 15 at the time of her arrest in March 1955. She was the first of the women to plead not guilty and request a trial. Mary Louise Smith was 18 in October 1955 when she refused to give her seat to a white person. Browder was a 36-year-old housewife when arrested in April 1955. And McDonald was in her seventies when she was mistreated by a bus driver.

The case was filed in February 1956 by lawyer Fred Gray. He had assistance from NAACP lawyers, including Thurgood Marshall. In June the U.S. district court ruled in favor of the plaintiffs. The following November, the U.S. Supreme Court affirmed that ruling. And on December 17, 1956, the Supreme Court rejected city and state appeals to reconsider the decision. It upheld the lower court's judgment that Alabama's segregation laws were unconstitutional.

4

SIT-INs AND
FREEDOM RIDES

In the South, racial segregation meant that managers of restaurants could refuse to serve blacks. It meant that water fountains and restrooms were labeled as for "Whites" or "Colored." It meant that whites and blacks did not share swimming pools, libraries, or other public places.

The SCLC, headquartered in Atlanta, Georgia, worked to end segregation in all areas of society. Campaigns to end discrimination involved lawsuits, boycotts of merchants, sit-ins, rallies, and marches. SCLC president Martin Luther King Jr., insisted on conducting challenges to segregation through nonviolence. This strategy of nonviolent resistance would help draw many members—black and white—into the civil rights movement.

TARGETING LUNCH COUNTERS

The strategy of nonviolence would prove crucial in desegregating American lunch counters. In most places in the South, blacks could not sit at the lunch counters of local department stores or neighborhood restaurants. As a routine practice, these businesses refused to serve food or beverages to African Americans.

In 1960, four young black men—Franklin McCain, Joseph McNeil, Ezell Blair, Jr., and David Richmond—decided to challenge this discrimination. They were freshmen at the blacks-only Agricultural and Technical State University in Greensboro, North Carolina. On February 1 the four entered the downtown F. W. Woolworth department store. The business catered to both blacks and whites. But the luncheon counter was open only to whites. The four black men made purchases in the store. They then sat down at the lunch counter and ordered food.

The white waitress told the men that she could not serve blacks. The manager asked them to leave. But the four stayed seated. They quietly waited at the counter until the store closed. And they returned the next day. This time they were accompanied by about 20 more students, including four women. Local newspapers and TV news programs reported the story.

On the third day, there were approximately 60 people participating in the sit-in. Among them were several African American female students from Bennett College. On the fourth day, three white female students from Greensboro Women's College joined the more than 300 students at the sit-in. A similar protest took place that day at the nearby S. H. Kress & Company retail store.

As news of the Greensboro protests spread, students organized sit-ins in other North Carolina cities and in other states. In some cases, African American students were joined by white students. Civil rights activist James Farmer later explained the importance of sit-ins:

> They symbolized a change in the mood of African American people. Up until then, we had accepted segregation—begrudgingly—but we had accepted it. . . . At long last after decades of acceptance, four freshman students at North Carolina A&T went into Woolworth and at the lunch counter they "sat-in." When told they would not be served, they refused to leave and this sparked a movement throughout the South.

THE SIT-IN MOVEMENT

In Nashville, Tennessee, 22-year-old Diane Nash was inspired by the Greensboro sit-in. Nash had grown up in Chicago, Illinois. Until she transferred from Howard University in Washington, D.C., to Fisk University in Nashville, she had not experienced the ugliness of segregation. She quickly became an activist. With John Lewis, she organized the Nashville Student Movement (NSM), which worked for the civil rights of blacks.

Nash and other NSM members had been planning to hold sit-in protests in Nashville. When they learned of the Greensboro protest, they decided to hold sit-ins in the same retail businesses. She explained,

> When the students in Greensboro sat in on February 1, we simply made plans to join their effort by sitting in at the same chains. . . . We were surprised and delighted to hear reports of other cities joining in the sit-ins. We started feeling the power of the idea whose time had come. We had no inkling that the movement would become so widespread.

The sit-ins were nonviolent protests, but at times they attracted violence. White segregationists poured itching powder, ammonia, or other irritants on the protesters. Or they physically attacked the sit-in participants. When students were arrested, others took their place.

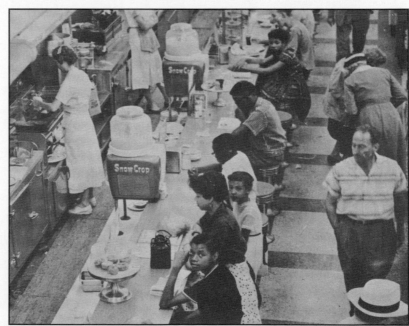

Young African Americans, probably students at North Carolina Central Agriculture and Technical College, conduct a "sit-in" at a segregated Woolworth's lunch counter in Greensboro.

The Day
They Changed Their Minds

Cover of a booklet about the sit-in movement, published by the NAACP in 1960.

Nash was in the middle of a particularly unruly luncheonette scuffle. On February 27 white teens attacked several protesting students. They were pulled off their stools and beaten. When the police arrived, only the African Americans, including Nash, were arrested.

"YES"

Fisk University professor Z. Alexander Looby was also an African American attorney who defended many of the Nashville student protesters. On April 19, his house was bombed by a bundle of dynamite thrown through the front window. That event brought Nashville's African-American community together. The next day more than 2,500 city residents and students, including Diane Nash, marched on city hall.

Mayor Ben West met the marchers at the city hall steps when they arrived. Nash asked West if he believed it was wrong to discriminate against a person because of his or her race or color. The television cameras were fixed on West when he answered with a simple "yes." The headline on the front page of the *Nashville Tennessean* the following day announced, "Mayor Says Integrate Counters."

The day after the march, Martin Luther King Jr. spoke in Nashville at a rally of Fisk University students. He said, "I came to Nashville not to bring inspiration but to gain inspiration from the great movement that has taken place in this community." Within three weeks, six Nashville luncheon counters no longer barred African Americans from service.

It took Woolworth's management much longer to change its segregation policy. Six months after the first Greensboro sit-in, on July 25, 1960, Woolworth officials ordered its store chains to desegregate. But the power of the sit-ins reached further. Similar protests that occurred in nine states eventually led to the passage of legislation that ended segregation policies in restaurants, theaters, and concert halls.

FREEDOM RIDES

In April 1960 Diane Nash and John Lewis attended a Shaw University meeting organized by SCLC official Ella Baker. A supporter of grassroots organizing and youth activism, Baker was reaching out to leaders of the sit-in protests. More than 200 students participated in the conference. From that meeting the Student Nonviolent Coordinating Committee (SNCC) was created. The student-run organization would go on to play a major role in coordinating sit-ins and other civil rights actions, including Freedom Rides.

Diane Judith Nash (b. 1938) helped to plan the successful Nashville sit-in movement. She later helped to form the Student Nonviolent Coordinating Committee (SNCC) in 1960, and organized Freedom Rides in 1961.

FAST FACT

When the retail stores Woolworth's and Kress agreed to integrate their lunch counters, Geneva Tisdale and two of her coworkers—all black kitchen workers at Woolworth's—were the first to be served.

During the spring and summer of 1961, more than 400 civil rights activists—black and white—traveled together on buses and trains on so-called Freedom Rides. Many were members of the SNCC. Others belonged to the Congress of Racial Equality (CORE), founded in 1942. Most were inspired by the work of SCLC president Martin Luther King Jr.

Committed to nonviolent protest, Freedom Riders refused to obey local laws mandating segregation. Such laws were supposed to be illegal. In 1946 the U.S. Supreme Court had ruled in *Morgan v. Commonwealth of*

THE TENNESSEE 14

Some of the first Freedom Rides carried students from Tennessee Agricultural and Industrial State University, now known as Tennessee State University (TSU). Eventually 14 TSU students would become Freedom Riders. Four of them were women. Many were arrested for breach of the peace and jailed. Because they participated in the protest, all the students were expelled from the university.

Catherine Burks-Brooks was born in Birmingham, Alabama. At TSU, she was a member of the Student Central Committee of the Nashville Christian Leadership Council (NCLC). Pauline Knight Ofosu, Etta Simpson Ray, and Mary Jean Smith were all born and raised in Nashville, Tennessee. They were also members of the Student Central Committee of the NCLC.

Ofosu and Smith were later reinstated in the school. Ofosu graduated in 1962, but Smith did not complete her studies.

Decades would pass before TSU recognized that the 14 students should have been rewarded, not punished. On April 25, 2008, the Tennessee Board of Regents overturned the expulsions. The university also awarded honorary Doctor of Humane Letters degrees to the students. On righting the wrong against the students, TSU president Melvin Johnson said the action would serve "to remind this generation of students of a time when young people were willing to risk reputations, careers, their freedom and their lives for a higher cause."

Freedom Riders sit on their luggage at the bus station in Birmingham, Alabama, May 1961. The Freedom Riders rode buses throughout the southern United States in order to draw national attention to local segregation policies that ran contrary to federal laws.

Virginia that was unconstitutional to segregate bus and train passengers traveling between states. That decision had been affirmed in 1955 by the Interstate Commerce Commission, the federal agency that oversaw transportation between the states. But in the South, local authorities continued to ban white and blacks from sitting together when traveling in buses and trains. The waiting rooms and restrooms were still marked "White" and "Colored."

In a 1960 case, *Boynton v. Virginia*, the U.S. Supreme Court overturned a lower court's conviction of an African-American student for trespassing in a bus terminal restaurant labeled for whites only. The Supreme Court affirmed that because racial segregation in public transportation was illegal, African Americans had a legal right to be in any restaurant or bus terminal that served insterstate passengers.

In the months following the *Boynton v. Virginia* decision, some African Americans decided to test local policies regarding segregation in buses and bus stations throughout the South. This was the start of the Freedom Rides. The first one left Washington, D.C., on May 4, bound for New Orleans. But its riders were brutally attacked and the bus firebombed in Birmingham, Alabama. Subsequent Freedom Riders also faced mobs of angry whites. Segregationists intercepted buses, pulled riders off, and beat them. Those who avoided attacks were frequently jailed for breaking local laws. Some were charged with breach of the peace.

John F. Kennedy had become president the previous January. His brother, U.S. attorney general Robert F. Kennedy had assigned John Seigenthaler to monitor the Freedom Ride protests. At one point, Seigenthaler asked SNCC leader Diane Nash to call off one of the rides. She refused, said Seigenthaler. She told him, "[W]e know someone will be killed. But we cannot let violence overcome nonviolence."

That September the Kennedy administration called on the Interstate Commerce Commission to enforce the ban on segregation in trains and buses. New regulations were drafted. And they went into effect the following November. The restrictions overruled any local segregation ordinances. Passengers were allowed to sit wherever they wanted on interstate buses and trains. The regulations also called for removal of "White" and "Colored" signs from terminals. Drinking fountains, restrooms, and waiting rooms were to be shared by everyone, regardless of skin color.

This was a legal victory. But the ban on segregated bus terminals was not accepted by all. And in November 1961 many facilities remained segregated.

5

LEGAL EQUALITY

In the spring of 1963, Martin Luther King Jr., and other SCLC activists went to Birmingham, Alabama. Despite desegregation laws and court orders, all its public facilities remained segregated. King wanted to bring Birmingham's racist policies to the nation's attention. He called for boycotts against businesses. Activists organized sit-ins and protest marches. Children and adults were encouraged to take part. By early May, hundreds had been arrested.

The Birmingham protesters were met with force. Firemen battered them with high-pressure streams of water from fire hoses. Law enforcement officers set police dogs on crowds. Police pummeled individuals with clubs. Photographs and television footage of the attacks on peaceful protesters horrified most of the country.

RIGHTING WRONGS

Appalled by the violence in Birmingham, President John Kennedy addressed the country on national television. On June 11, 1963, he called for federal legislation that would ensure all citizens, regardless of color, received equal treatment under the law. Kennedy said,

> I am . . . asking the Congress to enact legislation giving all Americans the right to be served in facilities which are open to the public—hotels, restaurants, theaters, retail stores, and similar establishments. . . . I am also asking Congress to authorize the Federal government to participate more fully in lawsuits designed to end segregation in public education.

MARCH ON WASHINGTON

Soon after, King and several other activists began planning a march on the U.S. capital. The only woman among the organizers of the "March on Washington for Jobs and Freedom" was Anna Arnold Hedgeman. She was a member of the National Council of Churches, a coalition of religious groups active in the civil rights movement. Hedgeman asked that women be scheduled to speak at the event. Instead, the executive committee decided that six prominent women of the civil rights movement would be acknowledged. They included Rosa Parks, Daisy Bates, and Diane Nash.

On August 28, 1963, more than 250,000 people came to Washington, D.C. The multiracial group marched from the Washington Monument to the Lincoln Memorial. At the steps of the Memorial, they listened to opera star Marian Anderson and gospel singer Mahalia Jackson. They heard several men, representing various civil rights organizations, give speeches. The one that would be best remembered was delivered by King. That day he gave his "I Have a Dream" speech.

During the program, Daisy Bates was asked to say a few words. In her short, unscheduled talk, she vowed:

> The women of this country . . . pledge to you . . . that we will join hands with you as women of this country. We will walk until we are free, until we can walk to any school and take our children to any school in the United States. And we will sit in, and we will kneel in, and we will lie in if necessary until every Negro in America can vote. This we pledge as the women of America.

Thousands of women were among the approximately 250,000 people who participated in the March on Washington, August 28, 1963.

Another woman who briefly spoke that day was celebrity entertainer Josephine Baker. But no women in the movement delivered a major speech. Nor was a woman a part of the delegation of civil rights leaders that met later that day with President Kennedy in the White House.

FREEDOM SUMMER

A year after the March on Washington, African American women were part of a major effort to register voters in the South. In the early 1960s many Southern blacks were denied the right to register and vote. This was par-

Council
Of
Federated
Organizations

9698 MAR-4 '64

1017 Lynch Street

P.O. Box 2896

(601) 352-9605

Jackson, Mississippi 39203

March 1, 1964

Aaron Henry
President

Robert Moses
Program Director

David Dennis
Assistant Program Director

Congressional District Coordinators

Frank Smith, 1st
Columbus

James Jones, 2nd
Greenwood

Jesse Harris, 3rd
Vicksburg

Matteo Suarez 4th
Meridian

Lawrence Guyot, 5th
Hattiesburg

State Office Coordinator
Charles Cobb, Jackson

Welfare and Relief Committee
Vera Pigee, Clarksdale
Annelle Ponder, Greenwood

Political Program Committee
Lawrence G Guyot, Hattiesburg

Finance Committee
Rev. R. L. T. Smith, Jackson

Federal Programs Committee
Jesse Morris, Jackson

Mr. Roy Wilkins, Executive Secretary
National Association for the Advancement of
                    Colored People
20 West 40 Street
New York, New York 10018

Dear Mr. Wilkins:

Enclosed is a report of the Mississippi Freedom
Summer program drawn up by the staff of the Council
of Bederated Organizations (COFO), which is a federa-
tion of all the national civil rights organizations
active in Mississippi. Since the NAACP is an integral
part of COFB, I'm sure you are familiar with its program.

COFO is holding a conference on March 15, 1964, to
which it invites all national civil rights leaders, to
coordinate their efforts in one direction for the
proposed Mississippi Freedom Summer program.

It is extremely vital that you try to schedule the
afternoon of March 15, 1964, to attend the COFO
conference in Jackson, Mississippi, beginning at
11:00 a.m., along with other national leaders. James
Farmer, James Forman, Whitney Young and Rev. Martin
Luther King are also being invited in order to establish and project each other's views for working together
on a joint COFO project, and make all plans and decisions
in common.

Since a press conference is being called after the
conference, we feel it is imperative that all national
civil rights organizations be present in order that
the statements issued will be representative of our
program. We feel that your joint efforts together in
Jackson would lend valuable impetus throughout the
nation for the Mississippi Freedom Summer project.

The agenda for the COFO conference for each national

The first page of a letter from Robert Moses, Council of Federated Organizations's program director, to NAACP Executive Secretary Roy Wilkins regarding the 1964 Mississippi Freedom Summer project.

ticularly true in Mississippi. The state had the lowest African American voter registration in the country. In 1962, only about 6.7 percent of eligible voters were registered.

The reasons had nothing to do with lack of interest and everything to do with white officials putting obstacles in the way at every step. Potential black voters were charged expensive poll taxes. Or they were forced to take difficult literacy tests. Many who attempted to register to vote were threatened with violence. Their homes were torched. Some people were beaten or even murdered.

In the summer of 1964, SNCC activists set out to register as many African Americans as they could over a 10-week period. More than 1,000 out-of-state volunteers joined thousands of Mississippians in the voter registration drive. Most of them were young, college students. They were black and white, male and female.

The registration drive was part of the Mississippi Summer Project, which was sponsored by the Council of Federated Organizations (COFO). This coalition included four major civil rights groups: the NAACP, SCLC, CORE, and SNCC.

CITIZENSHIP AND FREEDOM SCHOOLS

The Summer Project also involved an educational effort. Volunteers set up 41 so-called Freedom Schools in the state. Volunteer teachers, many of whom were college students, worked with more than 3,500 students. They

FAST FACT

Septima Poinsette Clark was fired from her teaching position in the 1950s for refusing to renounce her membership in the NAACP. She went on to found Citizenship Schools. Clark has been called the "Grandmother of the Civil Rights Movement" in the United States.

were literacy skills. And they were taught the constitutional rights of American citizens.

The Freedom Schools were based on Citizenship Schools, established in the 1950s by Septima Poinsette Clark. The former schoolteacher understood that state laws requiring literacy prevented African Americans from voting. So she developed a course of study to teach adults how to read and write. The first Citizenship School was established in 1954 on Johns Island, South Carolina. Soon there were many others throughout the South.

MISSISSIPPI FREEDOM DEMOCRATIC PARTY

Another goal of the Summer Project was to organize a new political party. In Mississippi only whites were allowed to join the Democratic Party. In April 1964 the COFO formed the Mississippi Freedom Democratic Party (MFDP). Both blacks and whites could belong, but the majority of members were African American.

One MFDP founder was Fannie Lou Hamer. In 1962 she had joined the SNCC to help register African Americans to vote. In June 1963 she and her fellow activists were arrested in Winona, Mississippi. They had asked for service in a whites-only bus station restaurant. Arrested for disorderly conduct, the men and women were jailed and beaten. Hamer was blinded in her left eye, and her kidneys were permanently damaged.

But Hamer did not stop her activism.

Fannie Lou Hamer (1917–1977) speaks at the Democratic Party's National Convention in Atlantic City, New Jersey, August 1964.

She served as the MFDP's first vice president. And in August 1964 she and two other black women—Victoria Gray Adams and Annie Devine—challenged the Democratic Party's all-white policy. They demanded to be seated as delegates at the Party's national convention in Atlantic City, New Jersey. In her testimony before the convention's credentials committee, she vividly described the violence and discrimination faced by African Americans seeking to vote. Her testimony was carried on national television.

The MFDP's bid to win a seat at the convention failed. But it had an impact. Four years later, at the 1968 Democratic National Convention, the MFDP challenged the Southern politicians again. And it succeeded in seating an integrated delegation. Adams would later note, "We accomplished the removal of the wall, the curtain of fear in Mississippi for African Americans demanding their rights."

THE VIOLENCE CONTINUES

But in the summer of 1964, many blacks had reason to fear what could happen in demanding their rights. For years throughout the South, white segregationists had used brutal violence against blacks. It took many forms, from drive-by shootings to the firebombing of offices and African American churches.

On June 21, 1964, three Freedom Summer workers disappeared. One was a black man, James Chaney. The other two, Michael Schwerner and Andrew Goodman, were white. Their bodies were not discovered until August. Their deaths made national news. And the white public became even more aware of the dangers civil rights workers faced in the South.

CIVIL RIGHTS ACT

President John F. Kennedy did not live to see his proposal for civil rights legislation passed by Congress. He was assassinated in November 1963. His successor, President Lyndon Johnson strongly supported the Civil Rights Act. But it took several months of debate before it passed. Johnson signed the bill on July 2, 1964.

The Civil Rights Act of 1964 outlawed discrimination based on an indi-

Carrying American flags, people participate in one of the marches from Selma to Montgomery, Alabama. The marches were held to raise awareness of voting rights.

vidual's race, color, religion, sex, or national origin. The Act outlawed segregation in businesses such as theaters, restaurants, and hotels. It banned discriminatory practices in hiring, promoting, setting wages, and firing employees. And it outlawed segregation in public facilities such as swimming pools, libraries, and public schools.

THE VOTING RIGHTS ACT OF 1965

But additional legislation was needed to ensure voting rights for African Americans. Further public support for a federal law came in 1965, after local police brutally broke up a voting rights march in Alabama. On March 7, 1965, the 600 civil rights protesters began a march from Selma to the state capital of Montgomery. But they were attacked with billy clubs and tear gas. The day became known as Bloody Sunday.

On March 21, around 3,000 marchers led by Martin Luther King Jr., set out again. This time, participants in the Selma to Montgomery march were escorted by the Alabama National Guard. On March 25, when the marchers reached the state capital, they numbered 25,000.

The news media reported on the voting rights march. And there was growing public support to remove obstacles that prevented blacks from voting. That August, Congress passed the Voting Rights Act. It called for federal workers to register black voters. And it prohibited the use of the literacy test as a condition for voting. On August 6, 1965, President Johnson signed the Act into law.

As a result, the number of African-Americans registered

This monument honors two women who helped to organize the March 7, 1965, march from Selma to Montgomery. Alabama police beat Amelia Boynton Robinson (b. 1911) at the Edmund Pettus Bridge so severely that she lost consciousness. Marie Foster (1917–2003) was also badly beaten on Bloody Sunday. Both civil rights leaders later helped many African Americans register to vote in Alabama.

to vote soared throughout the nation. By the end of 1965, a quarter of a million new black voters had been registered.

As African Americans gained political power, many ran for elected office. In 1968 Shirley Chisholm became the first African American woman to win a seat in Congress. She was elected to the House of Representatives, from New York. In 1972 she ran for the Democratic nomination for president of the United States.

WOMEN IN THE MOVEMENT

In the civil rights movement, men were typically the principal spokespersons and decision makers. But women were essential to the movement, according to SNCC activist Unita Blackwell. "Women were the glue that held the Movement together as the upper glue that holds most things together in the community," she said.

Blackwell acknowledged the efforts of Adams, Hamer, and Devine as leaders. "Those women had influence," Blackwell noted. "Those women had wisdom. Those women had courage and that's why they came to the Movement. They were in those positions at the appropriate time and they never shirked the hard decisions."

THE VOTER EDUCATION PROJECT

In late 1961 U.S. attorney general Robert F. Kennedy presented the country's major civil rights groups with a proposal. They would receive funding from private donors if they agreed to shift their focus from protests to voter registration.

Although most of the groups did not cease their protest activities, they did place greater emphasis on voter registration. In April 1962 the groups' leaders established the nonpartisan Voter Education Project (VEP). Under the patronage of the Southern Regional Council (SRC), a nonprofit research group, the VEP coordinated registration campaigns for the SNCC, the SCLC, the NAACP, CORE, and the National Urban League.

The effort was hugely successful: At its beginning, only 1.4 million of the South's 5 million blacks of voting age were registered. By the end of 1964, the VEP had helped register almost 800,000 more black voters in the South. One of the grants the VEP funded was a voter registration project in Selma, Alabama. That venture helped lead to the voting rights march from Selma to the state capital of Montgomery. The Voting Rights Act became law a few months later.

Lyndon B. Johnson (left) signs the 1965 Voting Rights Act. Pictured at the right are Vivian Malone (1942–2005), who in 1963 integrated the University of Alabama, and Rosa Parks. Other civil rights leaders, including Dr. Martin Luther King and NAACP president Roy Wilkins, are pictured in the center.

But the women who were not decision makers were also important. They provided support for demonstrations, protests, and boycotts. They participated in sit-ins and marches. They were willing to risk arrest for their civil disobedience.

Many historians agree that social change would not have come about without the women. Civil rights activist and historian Julian Bond acknowledged their contribution. "There's a Chinese saying 'Women hold up half the world,'" he said. "In the case of the civil rights movement it's probably three-quarters of the world."

CHAPTER NOTES

p. 11: "I am a believer in . . . " William Lloyd Garrison, *No Compromise with Slavery: An Address Delivered in the Broadway Tabernacle, New York, February 14, 1854* (New York: American Anti-Slavery Society, 1854), 5.

p. 13: "Excepting John Brown . . ." Frederick Douglass, quoted in Sarah Bradford, *Harriet Tubman: The Moses of Her People* (Bedford, Mass.: Applewood Books, 1993 reprint), 135.

p. 16: "Our woman's movement . . ." Josephine St. Pierre Ruffin, quoted in Rosemary Skinner Keller, Rosemary Radford Ruether, and Marie Cantlon, eds., *Encyclopedia of Women and Religion in North America*, vol. 2 (Bloomington: Indiana University Press, 2006), 866.

p. 21: "Segregation of white and colored . . ." Earl Warren, quoted in James A. Curry, Richard B. Riley, and Richard M. Battistoni, *Constitutional Government: The American Experience* (Dubuque, Iowa: Kendall Hunt, 2003), 257.

p. 22: "Mobs led by . . ." A. B. Chandler, quoted in Robyn Duff Ladino, *Desegregating Texas Schools: Eisenhower, Shivers, and the Crisis at Mansfield High* (Austin: University of Texas Press, 1997), 125.

p. 26: "The movement of the . . ." Ella Baker, "Developing Community Leadership," quoted in Gerda Lerner, *Black Women in White America* (New York: Vintage, 1973), 351.

p. 30: "Back then, we didn't have . . ." Ros Horton and Sally Simmons, *Women Who Changed the World* (London: Quercus, 2006), 135.

p. 30: "[W]hen that white driver . . ." Rosa Parks, quoted in Wayne Greenhaw, "Parks Felt 'Determination Cover My Body Like a Quilt'" CNN, October 25, 2005. http://articles.cnn.com/2005-10-25/us/parks.green-haw_1_city-bus-claudette-colvin-white-driver?_s=PM:US

p. 32: "This is for Monday . . ." Juan Williams, *Eyes on the Prize* (New York: Penguin Books, 1987), 69.

p. 34: "The story of . . ." Martin Luther King Jr., *Stride Toward Freedom* (Boston: Beacon Press, 2010), 54.

p. 34: "We came to see that . . ." King, *Stride Toward Freedom*, 161.

p. 36: "They symbolized a change . . ." James Farmer, quoted in Jim Schlosser, "Greensboro Sit-ins: Launch of a Civil Rights Movement," *Greensboro*

News and Record. http://www.sitins.com/story.shtml

p. 37: "When the students . . ." Diane Nash, quoted in Williams, *Eyes on the Prize*, 129.

p. 38: "I came to Nashville . . ." Martin Luther King Jr., quoted in Williams, *Eyes on the Prize*, 140.

p. 40: "to remind this generation . . ." Melvin Johnson, quoted in "Tennessee State University: Honoring Our Freedom Riders," Tennessee State University, 2008. http://ww2.tnstate.edu/freedomriders/47.html

p. 42: "we know someone. . ." Diane Nash, quoted in Shelia Byrd, "'Freedom Riders' Recounts Civil Rights Era Crusade," *Detroit News*, May 15, 2011. http://detnews.com/article/20110515/ENT10/105150302/ëFreedom-Riders%C3%AD-recounts-civil-rights-era-crusade

p. 44: "I am . . . asking . . ." John F. Kennedy, quoted in Richard Reeves, *President Kennedy: Profile of Power* (New York: Simon and Schuster, 1993), 522.

p. 44: "The women of this . . ." Daisy Bates, quoted in Grif Stockley, *Daisy Bates: Civil Rights Crusader from Arkansas* (Jackson: University Press of Mississippi, 2005), 7.

p. 49: "We accomplished the . . ." Victoria Gray Adams, quoted in Yvonne Shinhoster Lamb, "Victoria Gray Adams; '60s Civil Rights Advocate," *Washington Post*, September 9, 2006. http://www.washingtonpost.com/wp-dyn/content/article/2006/09/08/AR2006090801780.html

p. 52: "Women were the glue . . ." Unita Blackwell, quoted in Brenda Joyce Edgerton-Webster, "The Tale of 'Two Voices': An Oral History of Women Communicators from Mississippi Freedom Summer 1964 and a New Black Feminist Concept," (PhD diss., University of Missouri-Columbia, 2007), 108.

p. 53: "There's a Chinese . . ." Julian Bond, quoted in "Women Had Key Roles in Civil Rights Movement," MSNBC.MSN, October 29, 2005. http://www.msnbc.msn.com/id/9862643/ns/us_news-life

p. 56: "In every campaign . . ." Martin Luther King Jr., quoted in Barbara A. Reynold, "Coretta Scott King, Martin Luther King's other half" *Washington Post*, October 21, 2011. http://www.washingtonpost.com/blogs/therootdc/post/coretta-scott-king-martin-luther-kings-other-half/2011/10/20/gIQA2t853L_blog.html?wprss=therootdc

CHRONOLOGY

1896:   In the *Plessy v. Ferguson* ruling, the U.S. Supreme Court establishes "separate but equal" doctrine. Segregation is considered legal.

1909:   The NAACP is established; Ida B. Wells-Barnett is a founding member. For several decades, lawyers for the organization will work to end racial segregation through challenges in the courts.

1954:   Septima Clark establishes the first Citizenship School. On May 17, in *Brown v. Board of Education*, the Supreme Court of the United States rules that the "separate but equal schools" policy is unconstitutional.

1955:   On December 1, Rosa Parks is arrested for refusing to give up her seat to a white man on a Montgomery, Alabama bus. Her arrest for violating city law ignites a protest in the form of a bus boycott that begins December 5.

1956:   The Supreme Court final ruling on December 17 on *Browder v. Gayle* abolishes segregation on Alabama buses. The Montgomery bus boycott ends December 20.

Civil rights hero Dr. Martin Luther King Jr. once said of his wife, "In every campaign if Coretta was not with me, she was only a heartbeat away." After King's assassination in 1968, Coretta Scott King (1927–2006) took on a prominent role in the civil rights movement, and also worked for women's rights and world peace.

1957: In February, the Southern Christian Leadership Conference (SCLC) is founded. On September 4, nine black students are blocked by the Arkansas National Guard from entering Little Rock Central High School. On September 23, federal troops escort them into the school.

1960: On February 1, four college students begin a sit-in at a segregated lunch counter at the F.W. Woolworth's store in Greensboro, North Carolina. In April, the Student Nonviolent Coordinating Committee is founded.

1961: On May 4, the first Freedom Ride buses leave Washington, D.C.

1962: The Voter Education Project (VEP) is established.

1963: On August 28, approximately 250,000 people take part in the March on Washington for Jobs and Freedom.

1964: Volunteers register African American voters during Mississippi Freedom Summer. On July 2, President Lyndon Johnson signs the Civil Rights Act of 1964 into law.

1965: On August 6, the Voting Rights Act, which outlaws discriminatory voting practices, becomes law.

During the 1870s and 1880s, many southern states enacted literacy tests as part of the voting registration requirements. Voters were often asked to interpret passages from the U.S. Constitution, as on the form at right. The purpose was to prevent uneducated people, particularly poor African Americans, from voting. Confusing instructions made it easier to reject their applications because of "errors." The laws typically made poor, uneducated whites exempt from such literacy tests if an ancestor had voted prior to 1870—the origin of the term "grandfather clause."

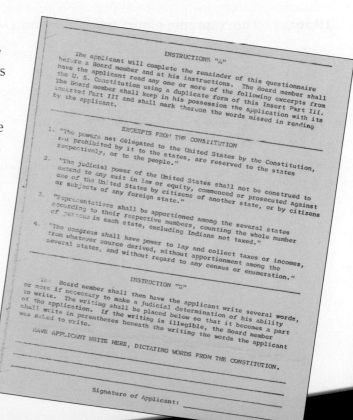

GLOSSARY

advocate—a person who argues for the cause of another person, especially in a court of law.

boycott—to join with others in refusing to deal with a person, organization, or country, usually to express disapproval or force another party to accept certain terms.

civil rights—the rights to political and social freedom and equality.

desegregate—to end a policy of racial segregation.

emancipate—to free from someone else's control or power; especially, to free from slavery.

integrate—to desegregate; to bring into equal participation.

lynch—to kill, usually by hanging.

memoir—a story of a personal experience; a biography or autobiography.

plaintiff—a person who brings a case in a court of law.

segregate—to separate or isolate a person based on his or her race, class, or group.

FURTHER READING

FOR YOUNGER READERS

Aretha, David. *Sit-ins and Freedom Rides*. Greensboro, N.C.: Morgan Reynolds Publishing, 2009.

Fitzgerald, Stephanie. *Little Rock Nine: Struggle for Integration*. Minneapolis: Compass Point Books, 2006.

Freedman, Russell. *Freedom Walkers: The Story of the Montgomery Bus Boycott*. New York: Holiday House Publishers, 2008.

Hardy, Sheila Jackson, and P. Stephen Hardy. *Extraordinary People of the Civil Rights Movement*. Danbury, Conn.: Children's Press, 2007.

Litwin, Laura Baskes. *Fannie Lou Hamer: Fighting for the Right to Vote*. Berkeley Heights, N.J.: Enslow Publishers, 2002.

Pinkney, Andrea Davis. *Let It Shine: Stories of Black Women Freedom Fighters*. New York: Harcourt Children's Books, 2000.

FOR OLDER READERS

Bradford, Sarah. *Harriet Tubman: The Moses of Her People*. Bedford, Mass.: Applewood Books, 1993.

Horton, Ros, and Sally Simmons. *Women Who Changed the World*. London: Quercus, 2006.

Keller, Rosemary Skinner et al., eds., *Encyclopedia of Women and Religion in North America*. Bloomington: Indiana University Press, 2006.

Stockley, Grif. *Daisy Bates: Civil Rights Crusader from Arkansas*. Jackson: University Press of Mississippi, 2005.

INTERNET RESOURCES

http://www.jimcrowhistory.org/history/creating.htm

This site links to several essays on American society during the Jim Crow years. It also gives various individual's perspectives on how Jim Crow affected their lives.

http://www.loc.gov/exhibits/brown/

Hosted by the Library of Congress, this website revisits the *Brown v. Board of Education* ruling. The site features photos of people and documents relating to the years before and after the 1954 order to desegregate public schools.

http://www.morethanabusride.org

The website for the film *More Than a Bus Ride* provides background information on civil rights activist Jo Ann Robinson and the women plaintiffs in the class action lawsuit *Browder v. Gayle*.

http://www.pbs.org/wgbh/amex/eyesontheprize

Based on the PBS American Experience television series *Eyes on the Prize: America's Civil Rights Movement 1954–1985*, this site links to profiles on people and documents from the time.

http://www.pbs.org/wnet/jimcrow

This website provides background information on segregation in the United States and Jim Crow laws. Includes maps and activities.

http://www.rosaparks.org

This official website of the Rosa and Raymond Parks Institute for Self Development provides information on the institute and a detailed biography of Rosa Parks.

http://myloc.gov/Exhibitions/naacp/Pages/Default.aspx

The Library of Congress exhibition *The NAACP: A Century in the Fight for Freedom* provides information about the women and men who helped shape the organization during its first 100 years.

Publisher's Note: The Web sites listed on these pages were active at the time of publication. The publisher is not responsible for Web sites that have changed their address or discontinued operation since the date of publication.

INDEX

Numbers in **bold italics** refer to captions.

CONTRIBUTORS

JUDY HASDAY, a native of Philadelphia, received her B.A. in communications and her EdM in instructional technologies from Temple University. Ms. Hasday has written dozens of books for young adults, including the New York Public Library "Books for the Teen Age" award winners *James Earl Jones* (1999) and *The Holocaust* (2003), and the National Social Studies Council "2001 Notable Social Studies Trade Book for Young People" award winner, *Extraordinary Women Athletes.* Her free time is devoted to photography, travel, volunteerism, and her pets: cat Sassy and three and three birds, Brandy, Rio, and Keats.

Senior Consulting Editor **A. PAGE HARRINGTON** is executive director of the Sewall-Belmont House and Museum, on Capitol Hill in Washington, D.C. The Sewall-Belmont House celebrates women's progress toward equality—and explores the evolving role of women and their contributions to society—through educational programs, tours, exhibits, research, and publications.

The historic National Woman's Party (NWP), a leader in the campaign for equal rights and women's suffrage, owns, maintains, and interprets the Sewall-Belmont House and Museum. One of the premier women's history sites in the country, this National Historic Landmark houses an extensive collection of suffrage banners, archives, and artifacts documenting the continuing effort by women and men of all races, religions, and backgrounds to win voting rights and equality for women under the law.

The Sewall-Belmont House and Museum and the National Woman's Party are committed to preserving the legacy of Alice Paul, founder of the NWP and author of the Equal Rights Amendment, and telling the untold stories for the benefit of scholars, current and future generations of Americans, and all the world's citizens.